Rob Matthews

Janus

Gallery Joe, Philadelphia
October 11 – November 22, 2014

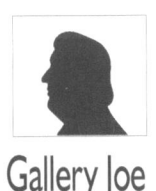

Gallery Joe

Front Gallery and Vault Gallery installation views

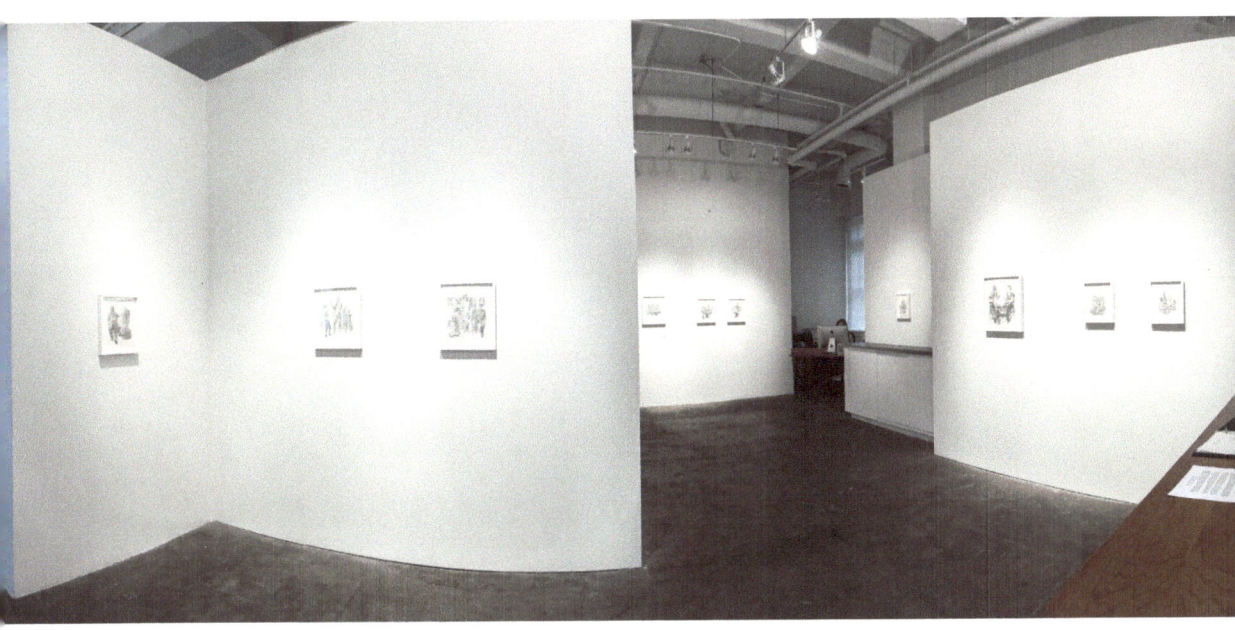

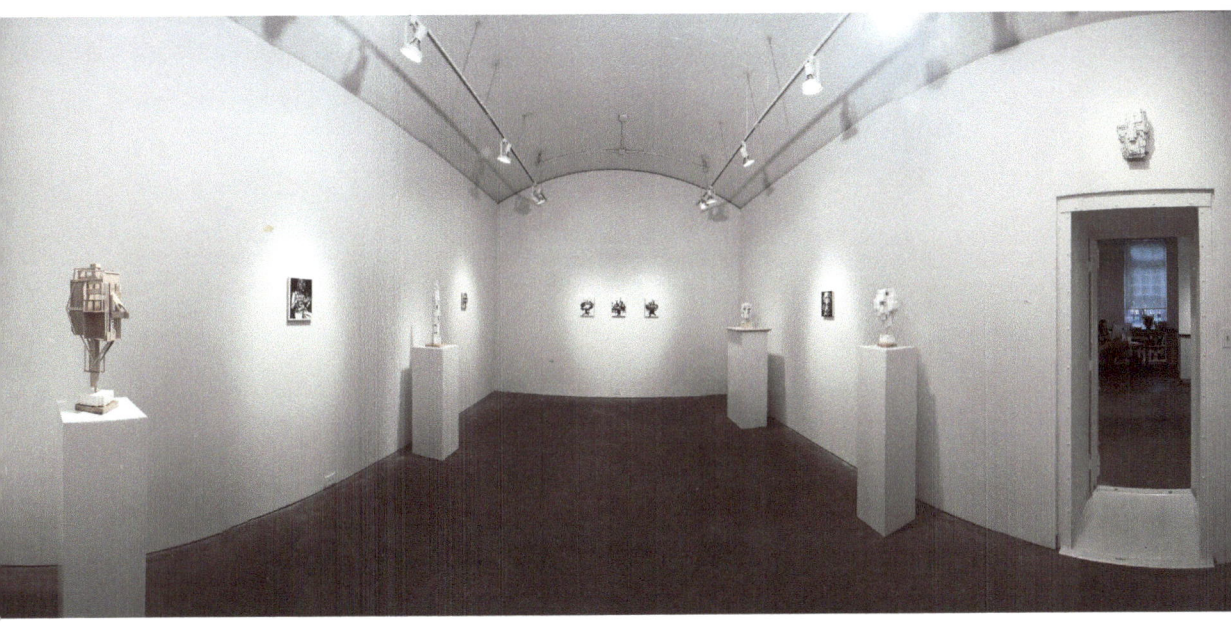

I moved to Nashville after living in Philadelphia for 14 years. It was not a blind move but a return to my childhood home. The process of moving was spread out over several years. In taking that long to formulate and engage a plan, I created a fracture within myself. Part of me was lost in the past while another part was planning for a future related to that past.

I was consumed with nostalgia.

What I was left with was an unhealthy desire to not be in the present, even if the present was a perfectly good reality. It was symptomatic of a larger spiritual void, a greater longing; what Georges Rouault defined as the "nostalgia for the infinite."

As a result, this work largely deals with time: linear, non-linear, finite and eternal. There are visible breaks, overlaps and collisions in space and time in line with the internal conflict that was at the heart of the creation of these drawings and sculptures.

In a number of ways, this is the most overtly personal work that I have made in years.

– Rob Matthews, 2014

Self-Portrait, 2013-14, Wood, spray paint, Approx. 11 x 7 ½ x 7 ½ inches

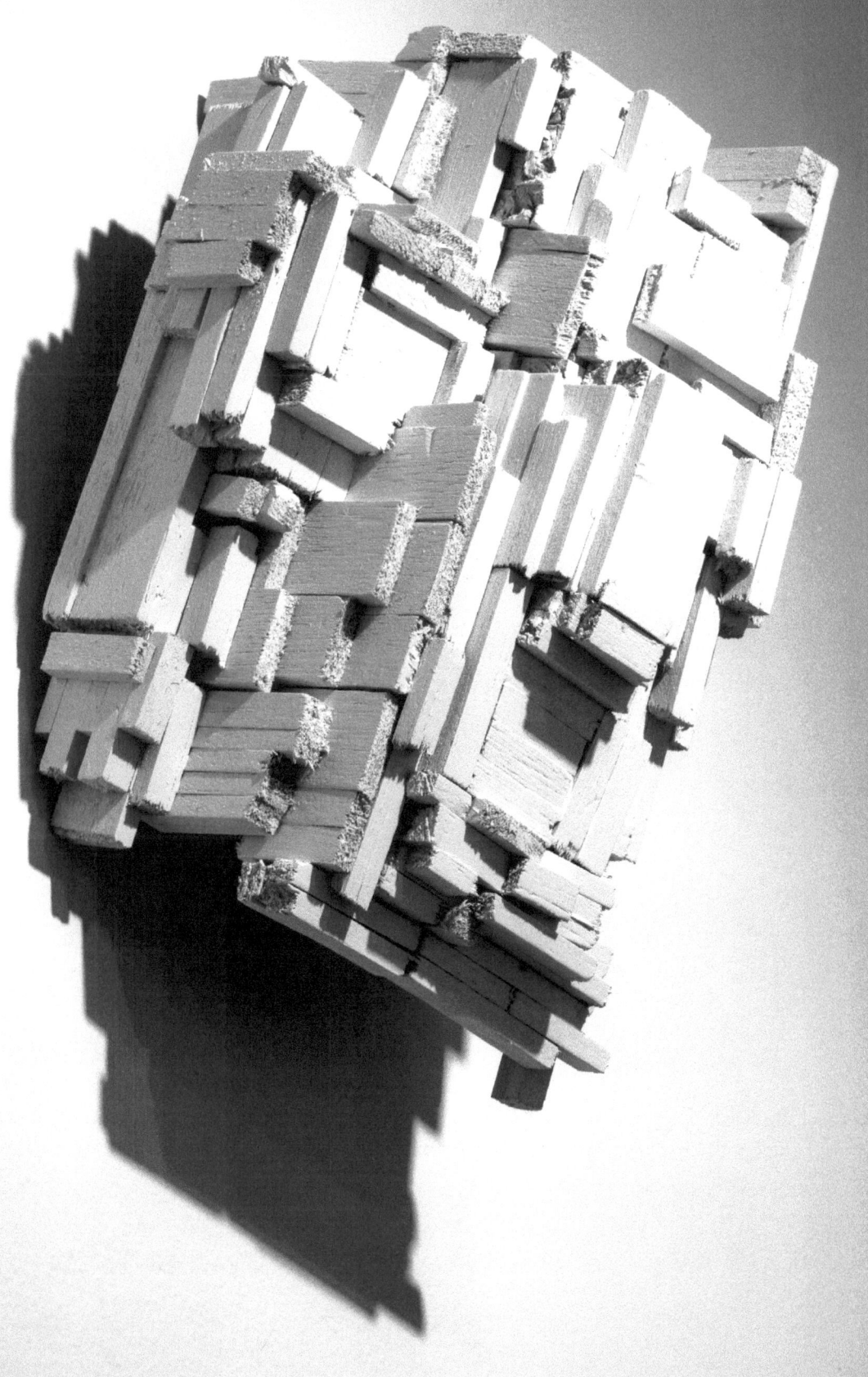

Prophets, 2013, Graphite on paper, 16 ¼ x 14 inches

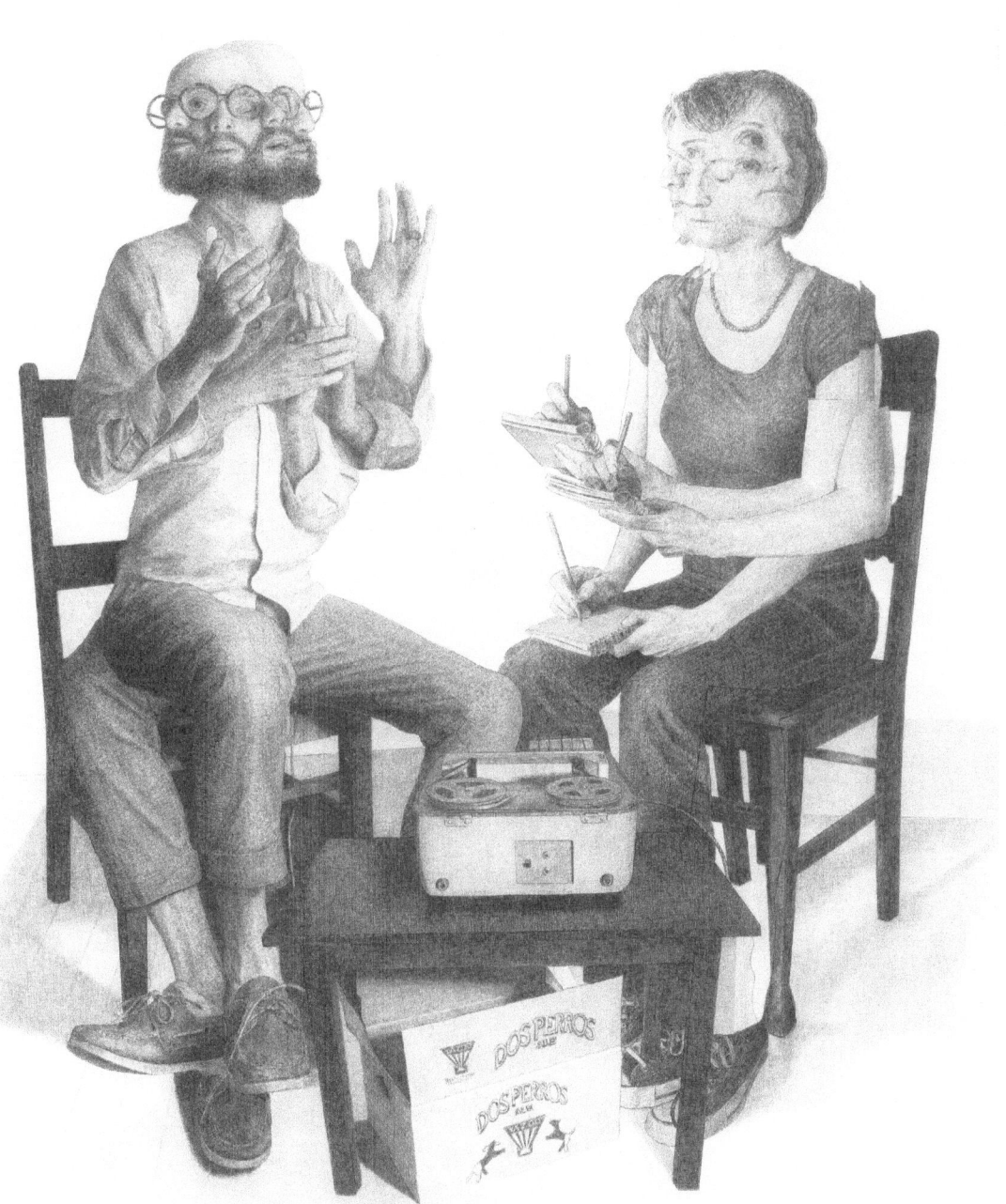

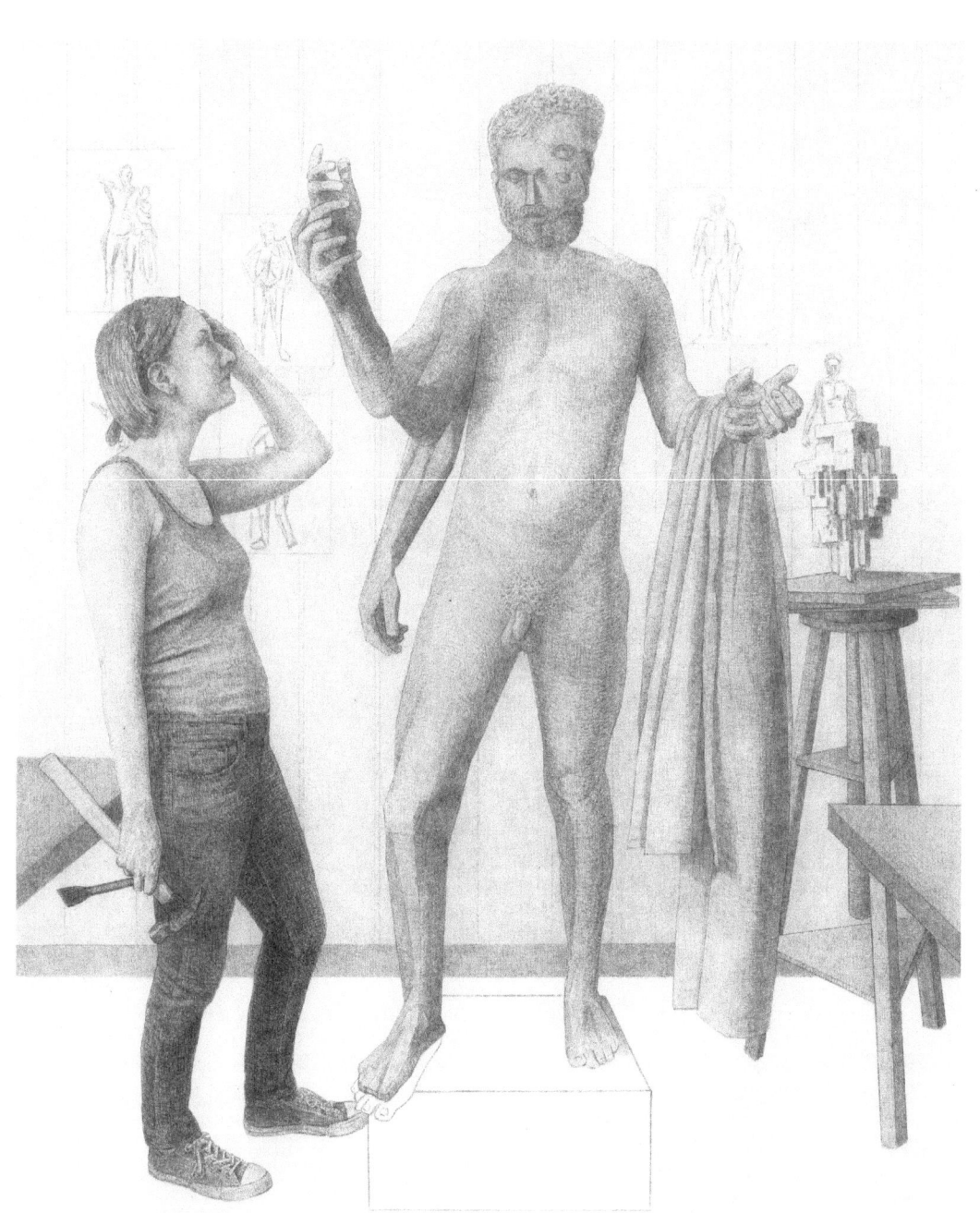

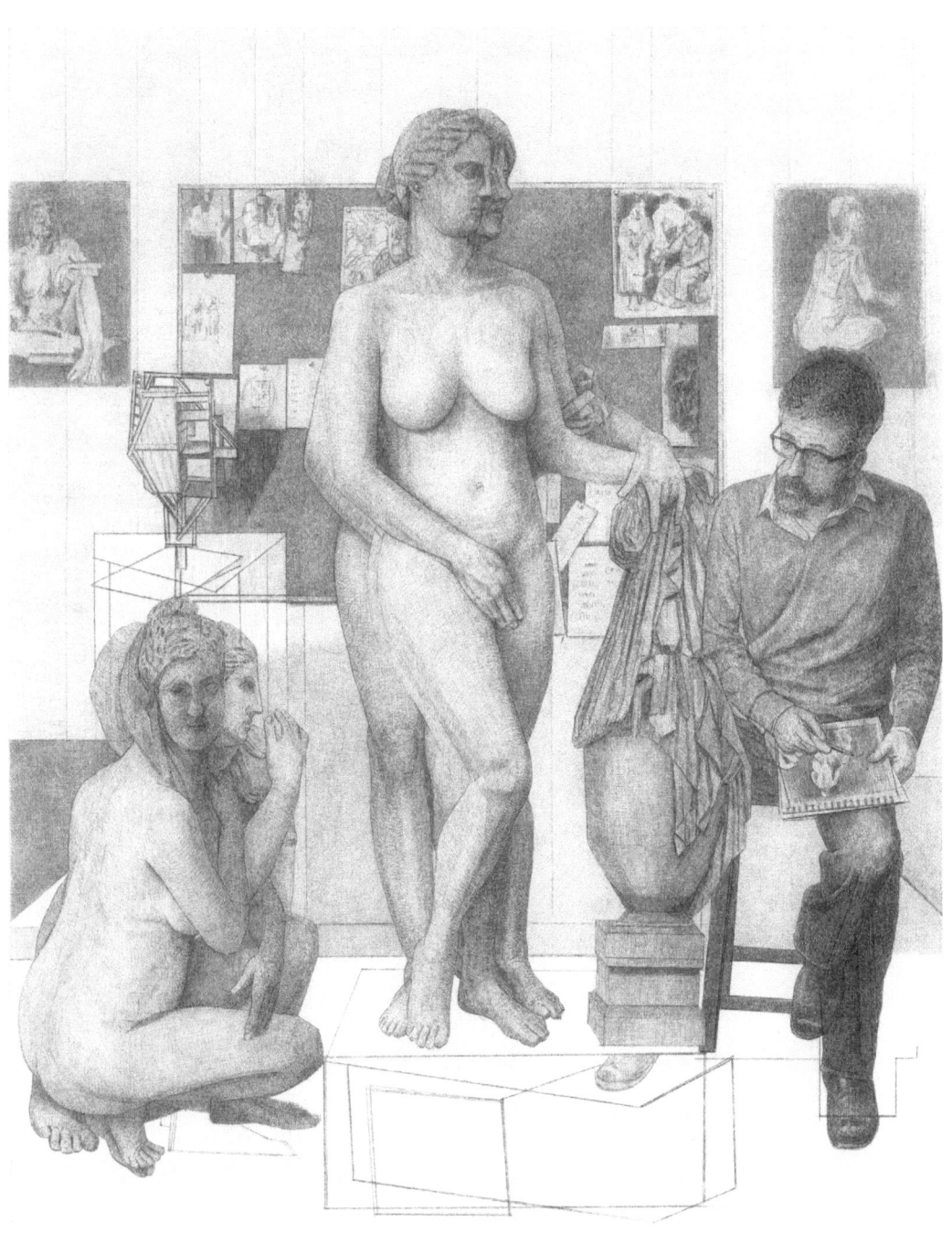

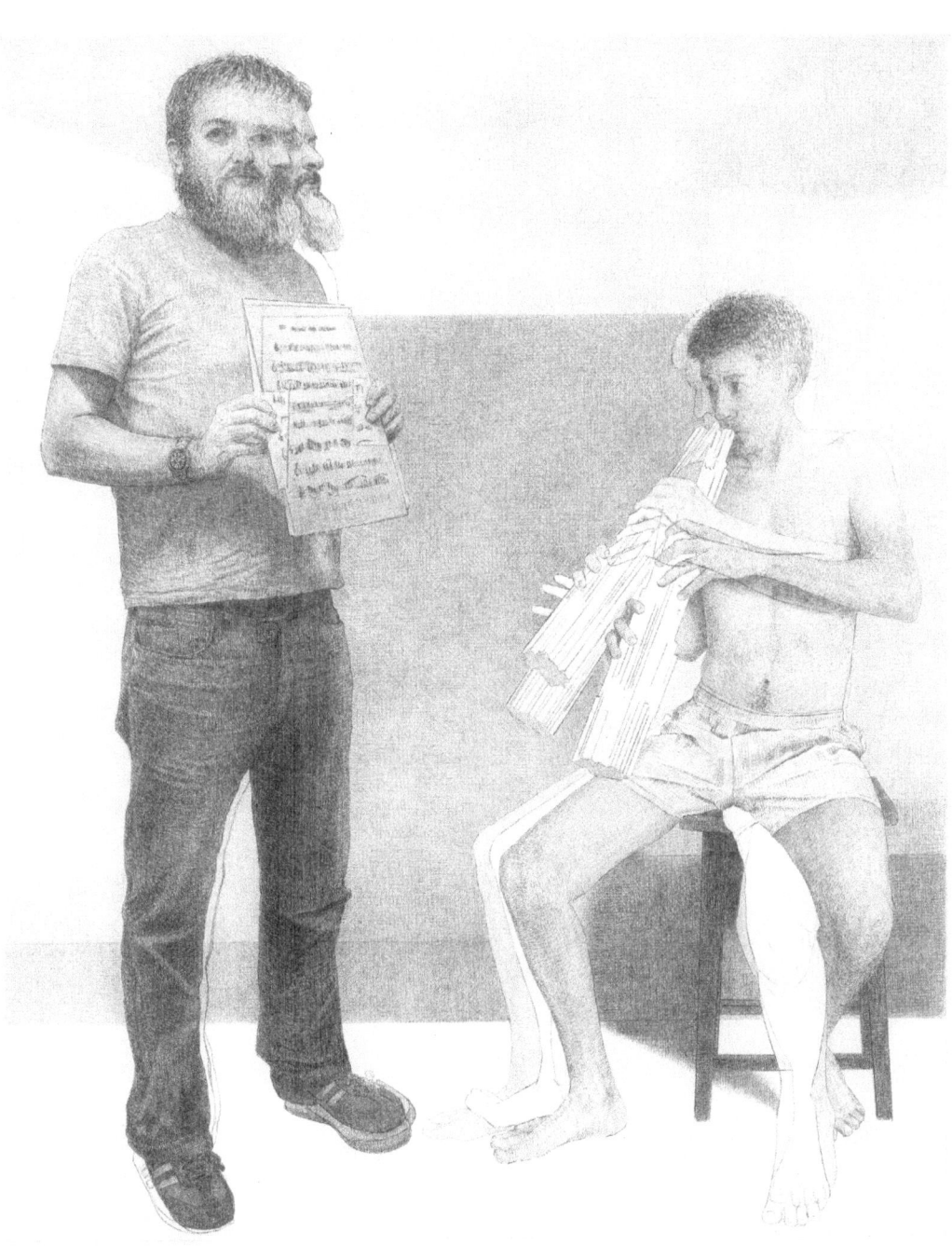

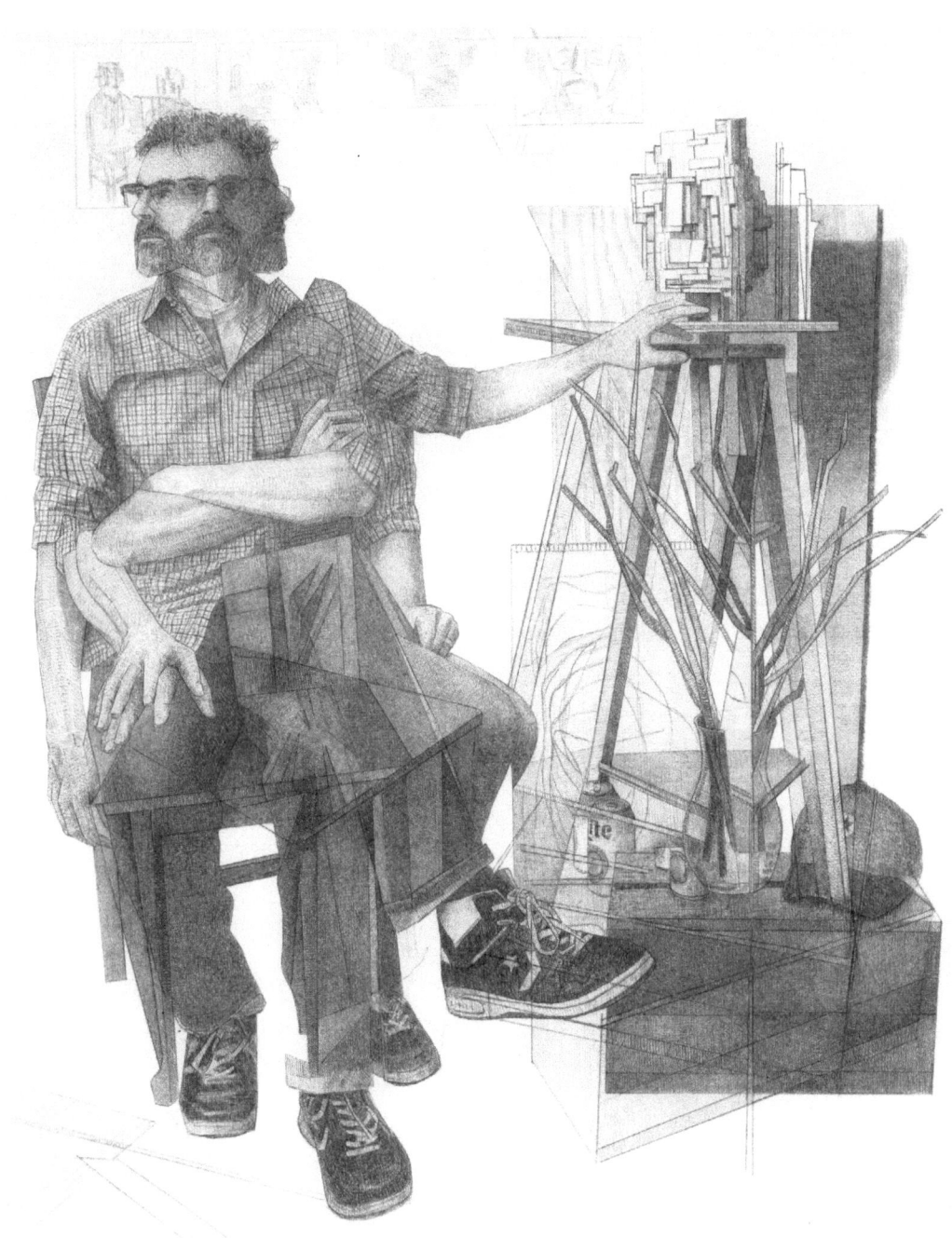

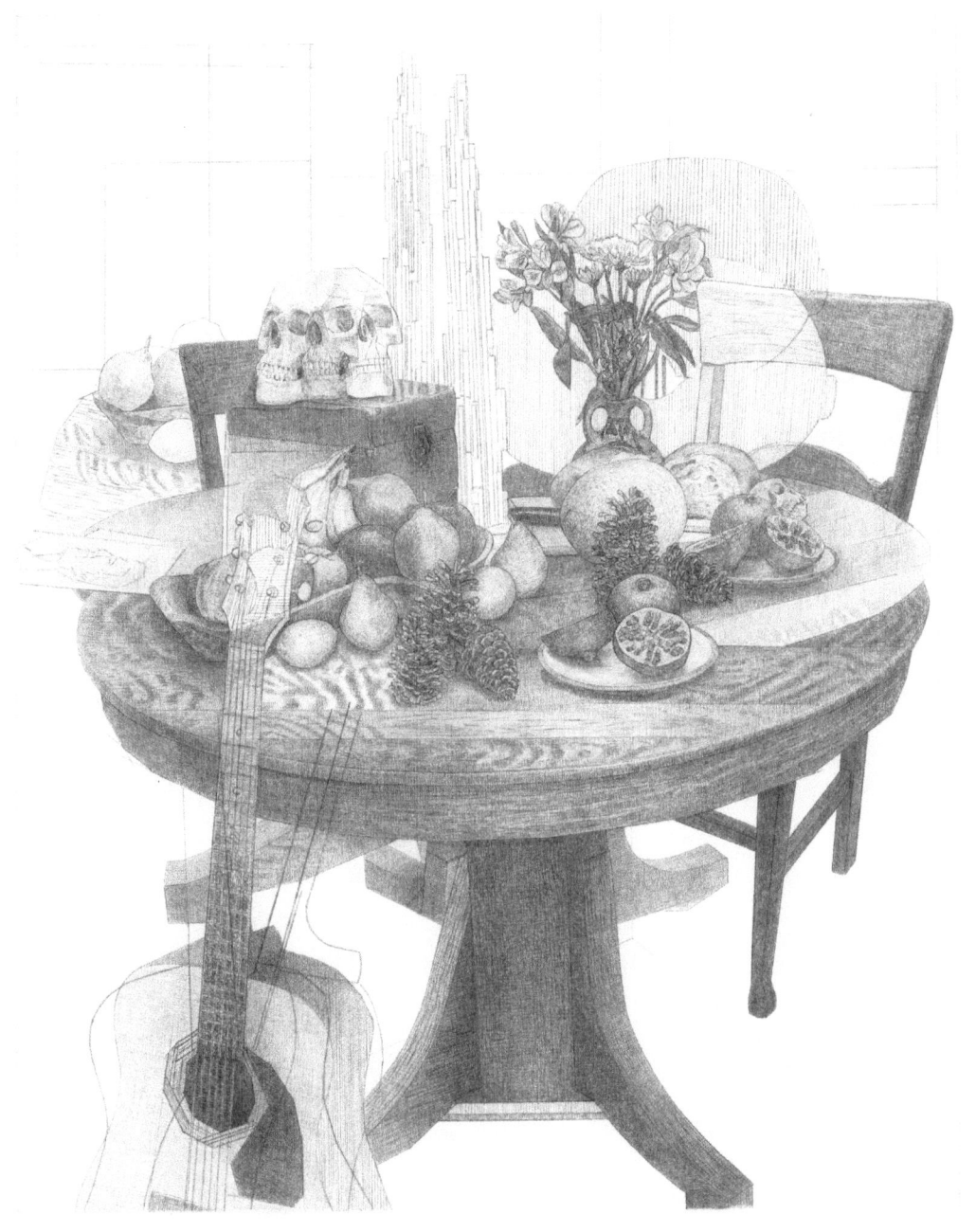

Still Life with Sheet Music, 2014, Graphite on paper, 13 x 11 inches

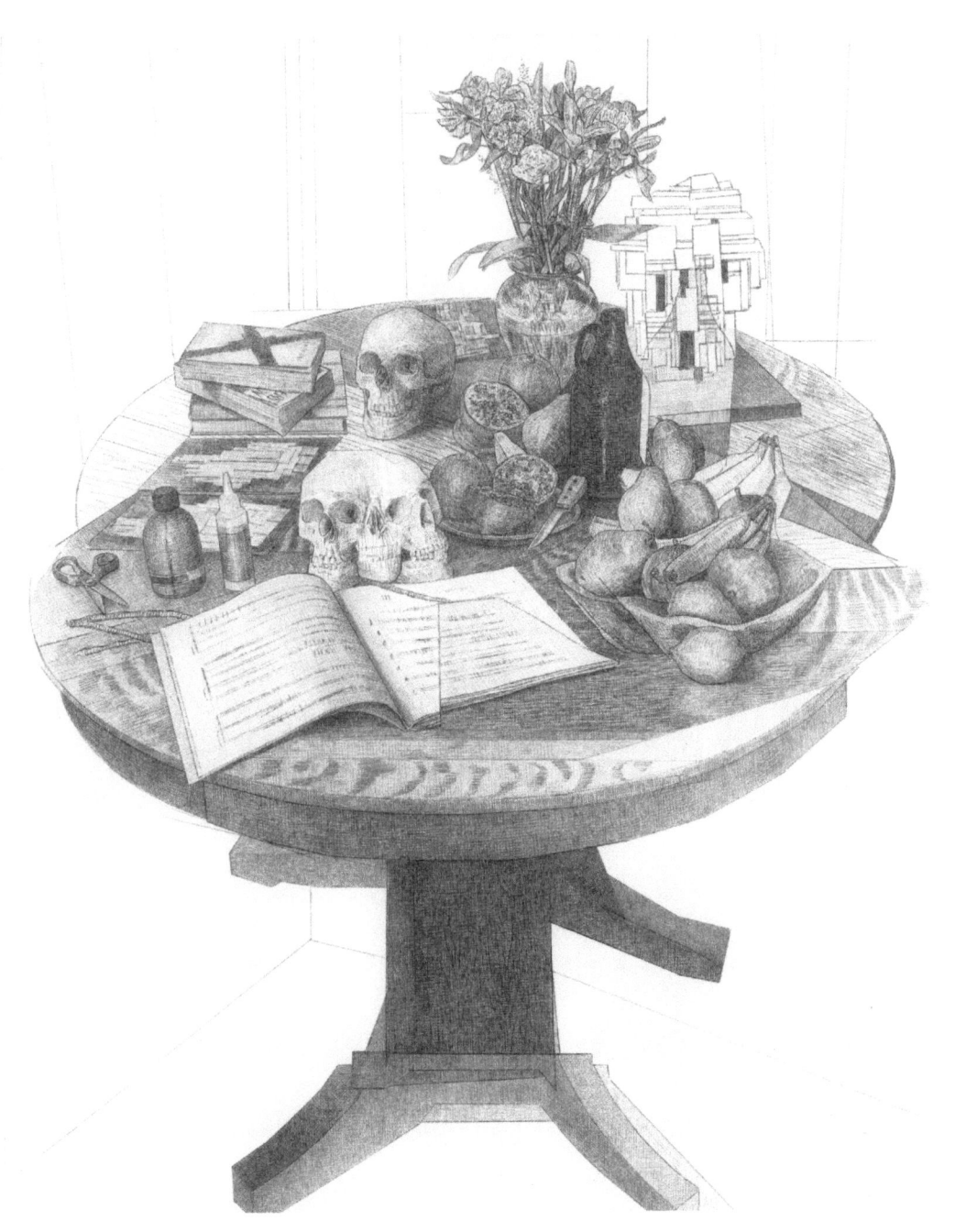

Still Life with Autoharp, 2014, Graphite on paper, 10 x 8 inches

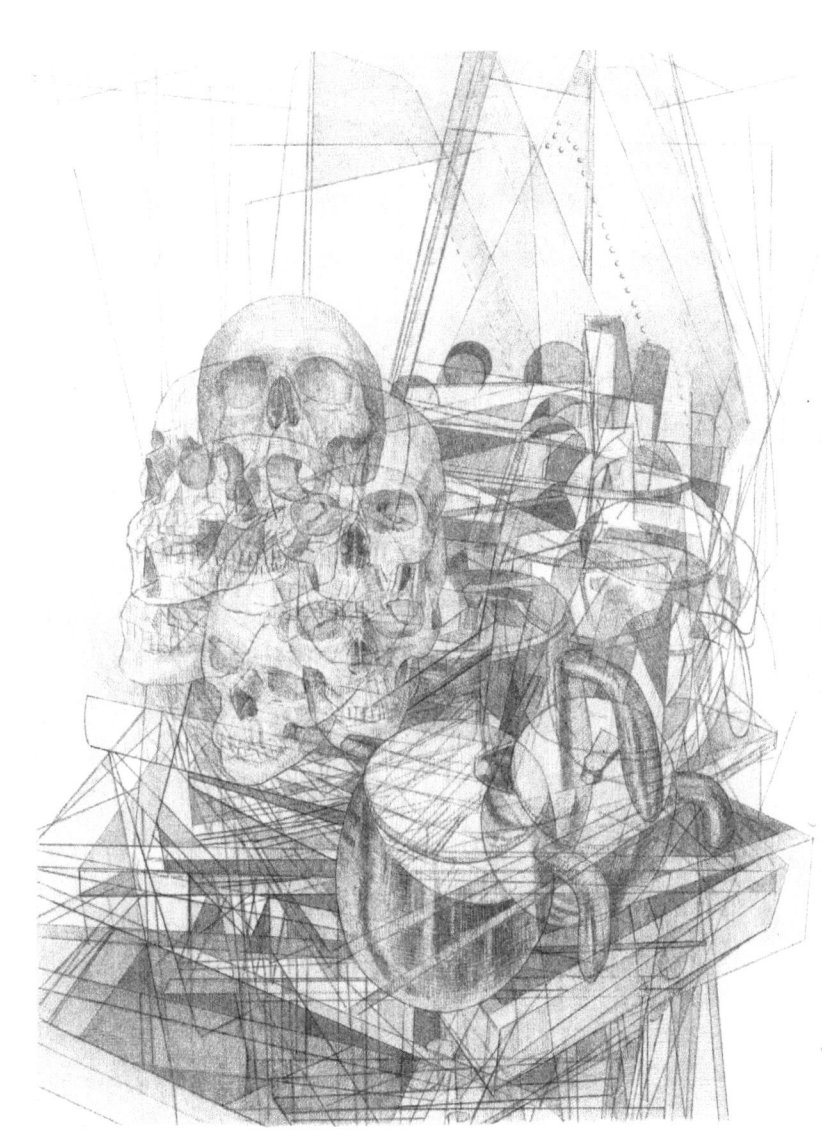

Tracy Crocheting, 2014, Graphite on paper, 10 x 8 inches

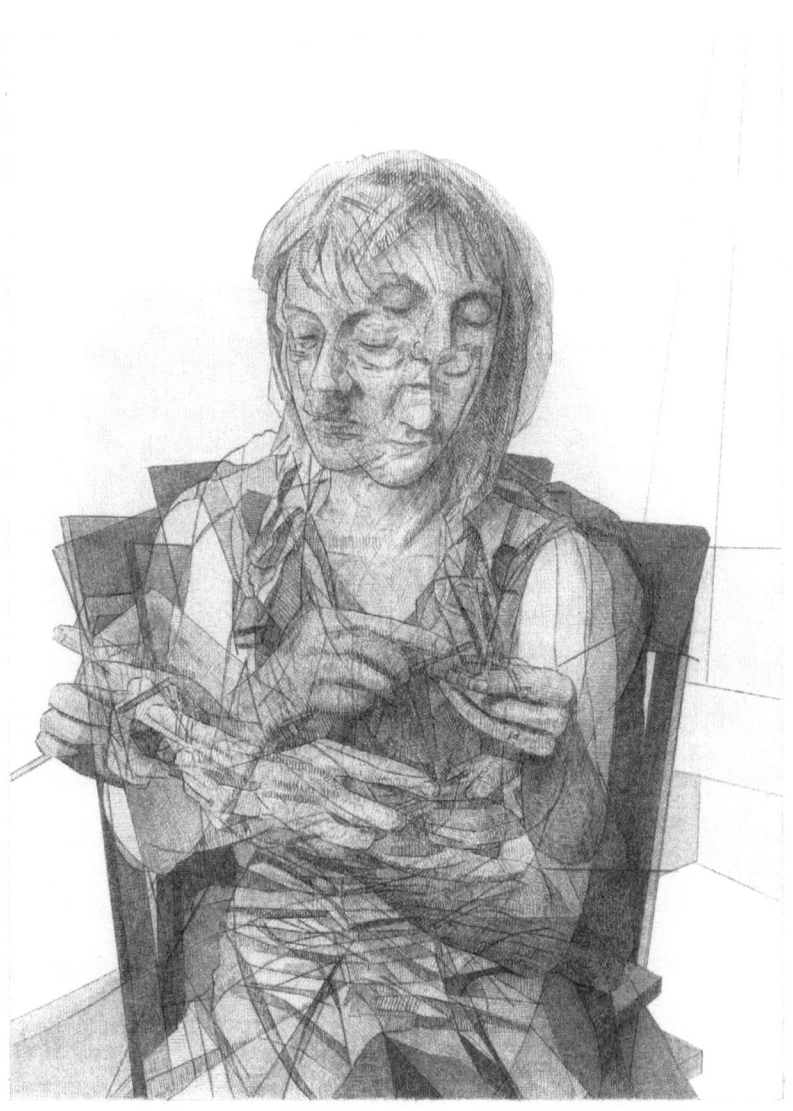

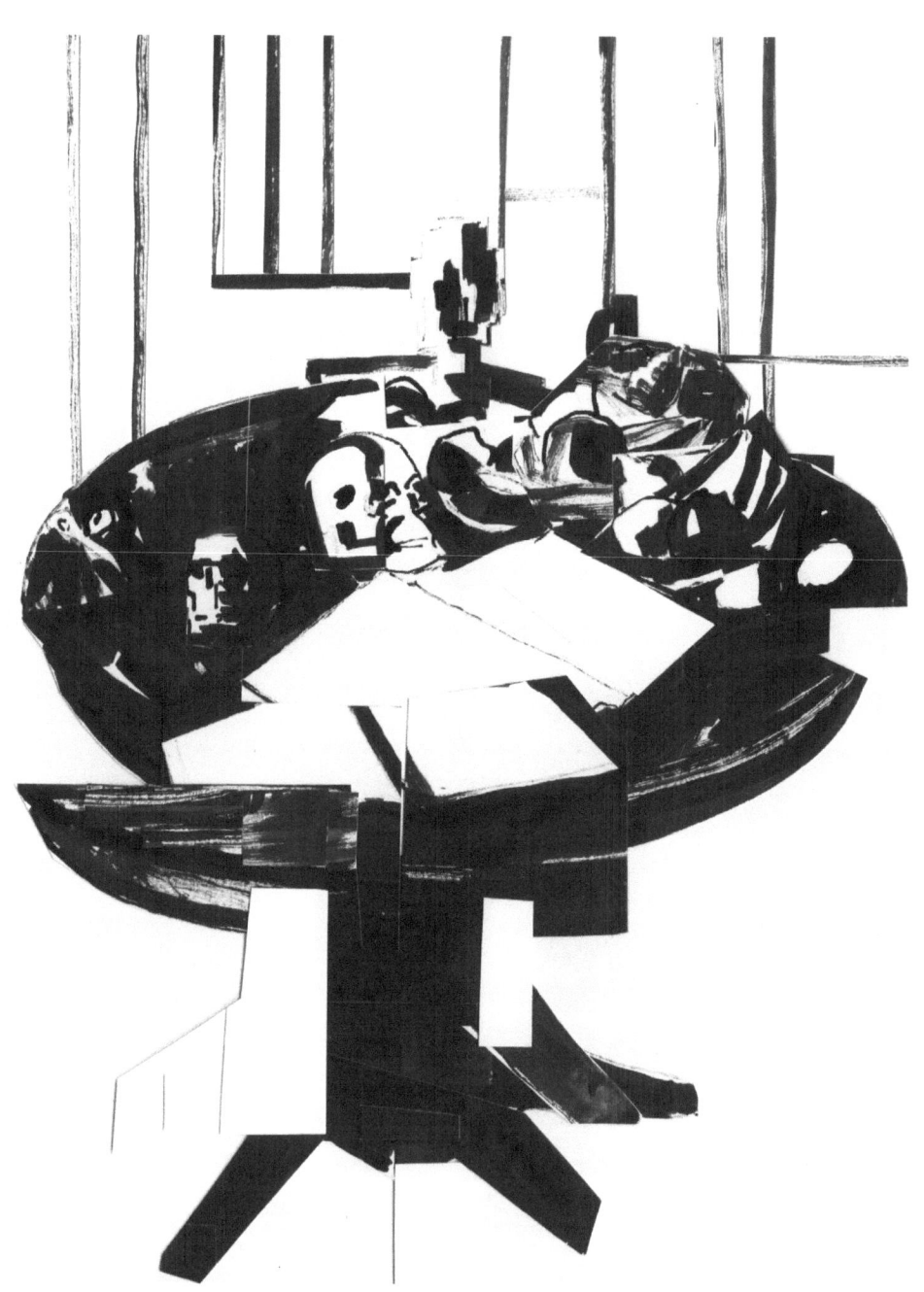

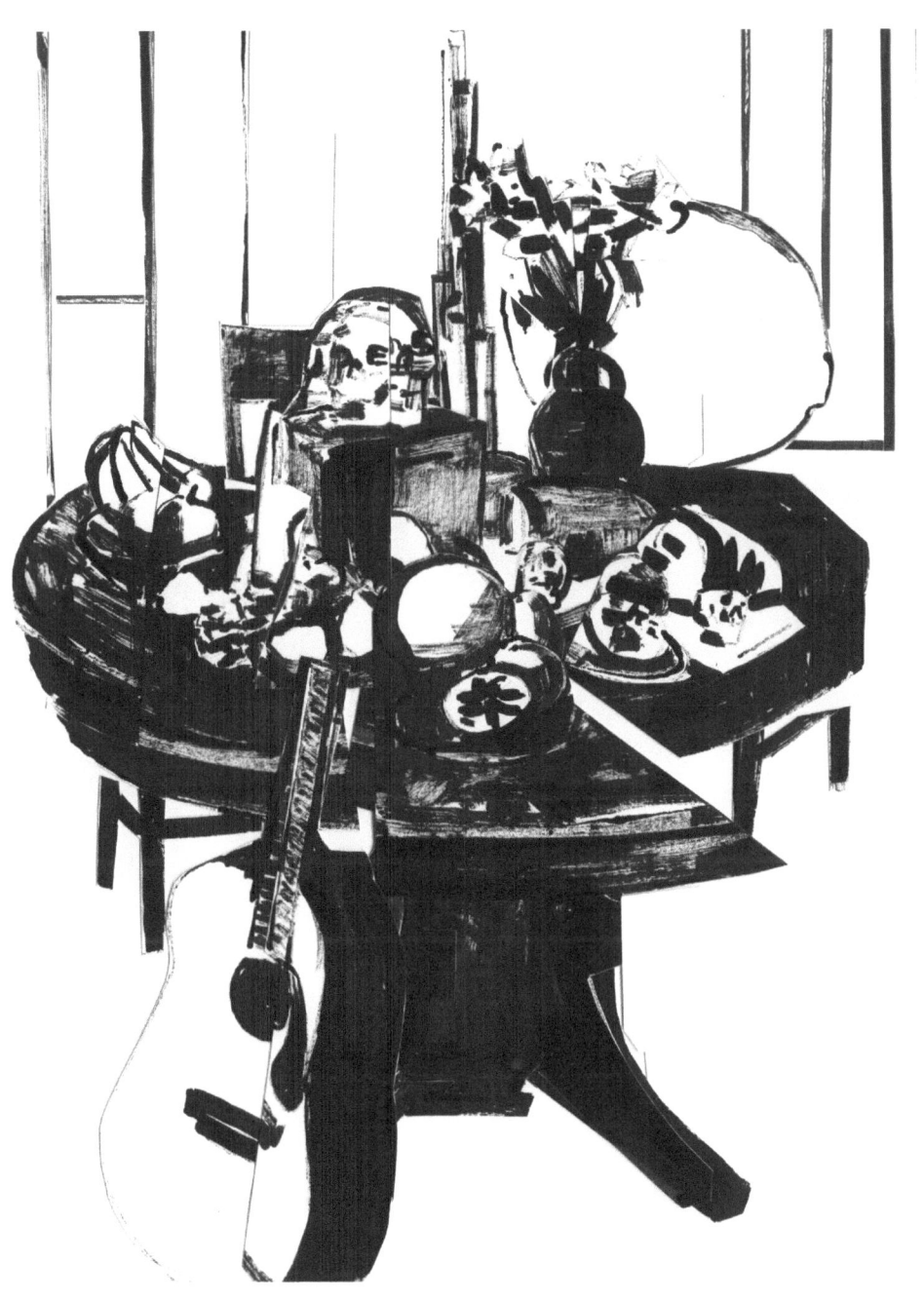

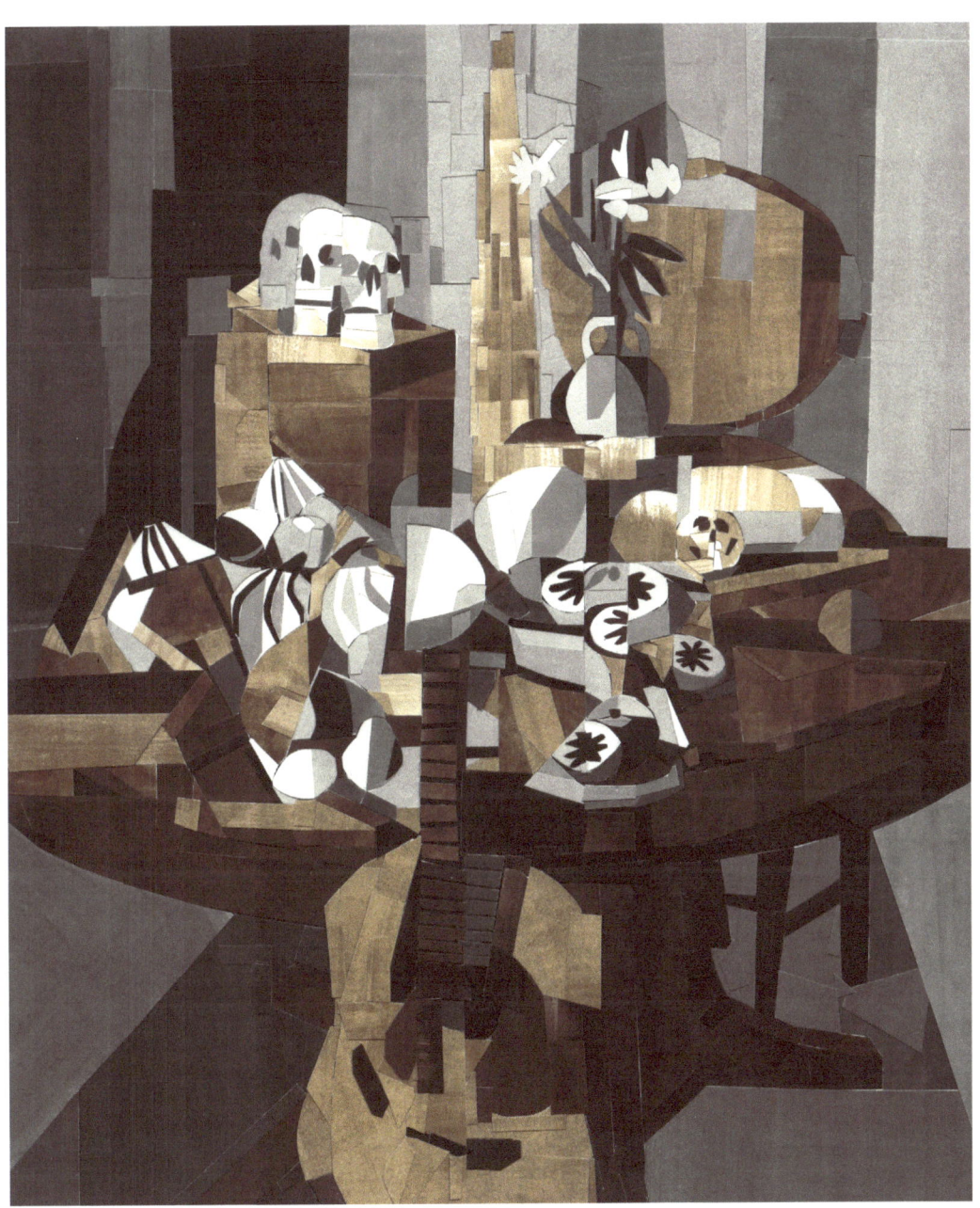

ROB MATTHEWS

b. Wilson, NC, 1974

Lives and works in Nashville, TN

Education

1999   Virginia Commonwealth University, MFA, Painting and Printmaking

1997   University of Tennessee-Knoxville, BFA, Painting

Awards and Grants

2009   PEW Fellowship in the Arts

2008   Pennsylvania Council on the Arts fellowship

2005   Finalist – PEW Fellowship

2004   Philadelphia Museum of Art Purchase Award – Works on Paper, Arcadia University

2004   Pennsylvania Council on the Arts fellowship

Selected Solo Exhibitions

2014   *Janus*, Gallery Joe, Philadelphia, PA

2013   *Life and Casualty*, Emory and Henry College, Emory, VA

        Drawings, O'More College of Design, Franklin, TN

2012   *The Middle Ground Vanished*, Daniel Cooney Fine Art, New York, NY

2010   *It Fills Us. We Arrange It*, Gallery Joe, Philadelphia, PA (catalogue)

2008   *Kindred*, Daniel Cooney Fine Arts, New York, NY

2007   *Knoxville Girl*, Gallery Joe, Philadelphia, PA, Anderson Gallery, Virginia Commonwealth University, Richmond, VA, Sarah Moody Gallery of Art, The University of Alabama, Tuscaloosa, AL

        18 Days, Raritan Valley Community College, Branchburg, NJ

2005   *The Assumption*, Gallery Joe, Philadelphia, PA

2004   *The Dumbest Man*, Philadelphia Art Alliance, Philadelphia, PA

Selected Group Exhibitions

2014   *Highlights*, Gallery Joe, Philadelphia, PA

2013   *Portraiture Now: Drawing on the Edge*, Arkansas Art Center, Little Rock, AR

        Passages, Daniel Cooney Fine Art, New York, NY

        Collection, Vox Populi, Philadelphia, PA

        The Search for Dispravosláviye, Tiger Strikes Asteroid, Philadelphia, PA

2012   *Small Scale: Expansive Visions*, Gallery Joe, Philadelphia PA

        Portraiture Now: Drawing on the Edge, National Portrait Gallery, Washington, DC

        Golden Beams of a Laughing Sun, Twist Art Gallery, Nashville, TN

        On Sincerity, 808 Gallery, Boston University, Boston, MA

2011   *Southern Cross*, Grizzly Grizzly, Philadelphia, PA

        Selected Drawings from the Allen G. Thomas Jr. Collection, Virginia Thompson Graves Gallery, Barton College, Wilson, NC

        Northern Liberties: A Transformation, Projects Gallery, Philadelphia, PA

2010   *The Pencil of Nature*, Julie Saul Gallery, New York, NY

        Still Life, Margarete Roeder Gallery, New York, NY

        Prints by Gallery Artists, Gallery Joe, Philadelphia, PA

        Philadelphia Story, Woodmere Art Museum, Philadelphia, PA

2009   *Casual Male*, Sherman Gallery, Boston University, Boston, MA

        Beautiful Human, Haverford College, Haverford, PA

        Contemporary Drawing Show, Elder Gallery, Nebraska Wesleyan University, Lincoln, NE

        Consequential, Addams Gallery, University of Pennsylvania, Philadelphia, PA

        The Philadelphia Story, Raritan Valley Community College, Branchburg, NJ

        My Certain Fate, Pharmaka, Los Angeles, CA

        50 Very Small Drawings, Gallery Joe, Philadelphia, PA

2008   *La Main qui dessinait toute seule*, Galerie Magda Danysz, Paris, France

        Sense of place, Gallery Joe, Philadelphia, PA

        ¡Fake!, Frieze Art Fair courtesy of Museu de Arte Contemporaneo de Castille Y Leon

        Vocabularies Of Metaphor: More Stories, Hosfelt Gallery, San Francisco, CA

        The Strange Place, Alogon Gallery, Chicago, IL

        Spot Check: Academy Contemporary, Pennsylvania Academy of the Fine Arts, Philadelphia, PA

        The Drawing Narrative, Jenny Jaskey Gallery at Tower, Philadelphia, PA

2007   *This Place is Ours!*, The Pennsylvania Academy of the Fine Arts,
       Philadelphia, PA
       The Blogger Show, Agni Gallery, New York, NY
       On the Mark!, Turchin Center for the Arts, Appalachian State University,
       Boone, NC
       The Diane and Sandy Besser Collection, de Young Museum, San Francisco, CA
       About Face, Gallery 817, University of the Arts, Philadelphia, PA
       Picture Journal Project, Woodmere Art Museum, Philadelphia, PA
       Center for Emerging Visual Artists, Philadelphia, PA

2006   *Everyday*, Pennsylvania College of Art and Design, Lancaster, PA
       Fine Line, Adam Baumgold Gallery, New York, NY
       Reconciliation, IAM Conference, Cooper Union, New York, NY
       Posture and Expression, Gallery 817, University of the Arts, Philadelphia, PA
       Recent Acquisitions: Prints and Drawings from Dürer to Doig, Philadelphia
       Museum of Art, Philadelphia, PA
       181st Annual: An Invitational Exhibition of Contemporary American Art,
       National Academy, New York, NY
       drawn, Art Murmur Gallery, Los Angeles, CA

2005   *Round the Gallery*, The Shore Institute of Contemporary Arts,
       Long Branch, NJ
       Adam Baumgold Gallery, New York, NY
       Torrid, Shardin Art Gallery, Kutztown University, Kutztown, PA

2004   *The Great Master*, Spector Gallery, Philadelphia, PA
       Sunday Afternoon, Match-Art, Brooklyn, NY
       Small Works, Gallery Joe, Philadelphia, PA
       Figure Out, Gallery Joe, Philadelphia, PA
       Wagons East, King Fisher Projects, Ridgewood, NY
       Works on Paper 2004, Arcadia University Art Gallery, Glenside, PA
       First Person, Gallery Schlesinger, New York, NY

Selected Public Collections

North Carolina Museum of Art, Raleigh, NC
Pennsylvania Academy of the Fine Arts, Philadelphia, PA
Philadelphia Museum of Art, Philadelphia, PA
de Young Museum, San Francisco, CA

Rob Matthews: Janus
October 11 – November 22, 2014

Gallery Joe
302 Arch Street, Philadelphia, PA 19106
215.592.7752
www.galleryjoe.com

cover image: *Still Life with Guitar and Pinecones* (detail)

Author/Editor: Rebecca Kerlin
Photography: Ken Yanoviak, Rob Matthews

Publication copyright © 2014 Gallery Joe
Image copyright © Rob Matthews

ISBN-13: 978-1503143135

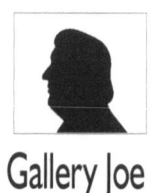

Gallery Joe

www.ingramcontent.com/pod-product-compliance
Lightning Source LLC
Chambersburg PA
CBHW050909180526
45159CB00007B/2840